D0567841

First edition.

LEARN CODING BASICS IN HOURS WITH SMALL BASIC

An Introduction to Coding for People with No Prior Experience

**Written by: Jack C. Stanley and Erik D. Gross,
Co-Founders of The Tech Academy**

PREFACE

The Tech Academy is a licensed career school that delivers software developer training. Our main offering is the Software Developer Boot Camp. The program can be taken online from anywhere or at one of our campuses.

Please keep in mind that this is the first edition of this book. There will be upgrades and revisions in the future.

If you find any errors, have feedback or would like to give suggestions, please contact us immediately. Our contact information can be found on our website: learncodinganywhere.com

Thank you for obtaining this book. We hope that you enjoy it!

INTRODUCTION

Welcome!

This book will be useful for individuals who are interested in learning coding and the basics of Small Basic. Don't worry if you haven't ever coded before though, this book doesn't require any previous knowledge or experience.

If you have written code before, this book isn't recommended because it was made for total beginners (people with absolutely *no* prior experience).

This book should be read start to finish, with all assignments completed in order. All tasks and code you are required to write herein are written in gray font. As a developer-in-training, you need all the experience you can get in typing code! So, definitely type all of the code in this book.

As this book is meant for newcomers, we won't start writing code until Section Three. The first couple sections we will be covering programming fundamentals and the required vocabulary. Please be patient because writing code without any understanding of the basics of coding is a waste of time and creates nothing more than a parrot.

The information presented in this book is arranged in a gradient sequence – we will start with the easiest information first and end with the most difficult tasks.

The purpose of this book is to create: *A programmer who understands the basics of coding and can write code in Small Basic.*

This book was written by The Tech Academy. We are a licensed career school that trains students in computer programming and web development. If you're interested in finding out more about us, please visit our website: https://www.learncodinganywhere.com/

Let's begin this book with some fundamental terms to orient you to the subject.

SECTION ONE
BASIC DEFINITIONS

Understanding the terminology of a subject is a vital component to mastering it. After all, how well could you drive a car if you didn't know what a gas pedal was?

So, while it may be boring, read through the following technological definitions so we can ensure a firm foundation is in place.

Note: If there are any technological terms you would like to clear up that aren't defined in this book, you can refer to The Tech Academy's *Technology Basics Dictionary, Tech and Computers Simplified.* This dictionary is available for purchase on Amazon.

DEFINITIONS

Machine: Something that uses energy to do things. Machines are most commonly made out of metal and plastic and have several parts that work together. They are usually made up of fixed and moving parts that each serves a particular purpose. Machines are used by people as tools to assist in getting something done.

EXAMPLE: A car is a machine.

Computer: An electronic machine that stores and deals with information. A computer is made up of many different parts through which electricity passes through. Computers are a tool that people use to help them do things.

Computers follow instructions entered into them by people. A computer can store instructions to be done at later points in time, so that people do not have to re-enter the same instructions over and over again. The computer automatically performs a series of functions when it is on and also responds to commands that a person enters into it. The way it responds to commands is all set up beforehand by people.

Machines, such as cars and phones, can have computers inside them that perform specific functions. Computers typically exist to help people by performing repetitive activities, storing information and making certain activities faster or more efficient.

EXAMPLE: An electronic calculator is a very basic type of computer.

Digital: Of, or related to, a device or object that represents magnitudes in digits. Computers are digital devices; data in computers is represented using digits.

The opposite of "digital" can be considered to be "analog." Analog refers to data flowing out in a continuous stream.

Things that are digital are made up of exact, distinct parts; these parts are always in an exact, standard state (state is the condition of a thing – for example, "green," "empty," "45 years old," etc.). Digital things can only be in one of the available states for that thing, and not "in between" two of the available states. For example, a light bulb with a regular flip switch would be digital because it has only two states: totally off or totally on. If the light bulb had one of those round dimmer switches instead of a flip switch and it could be set to somewhere between "totally off" and "totally on," it would not be digital.

A black and white photo that is created using only small black and white dots is digital. From a distance, you see the image that the photograph represents. If you look at it up close, you see that the photo is composed of individual small dots. The distinct dots are digital in that they are exact, separated marks.

EXAMPLE: In terms of physical universe objects, a staircase would be considered digital and a ramp would be analog. Stairs have distinct, separated steps. A ramp is continuous.

Computers are digital because they communicate using two numbers: 0 (which tells the computer "off"), and 1 (which tells the computer "on").

Note: People typically use the word digital to refer to anything that has to do with computers.

Central Processing Unit: "CPU" for short. The CPU is basically the "brain" of the computer.

A Central Processing Unit is the part of a computer that controls all the actions the computer does. It is a small device that contains billions of tiny electronic components.

Most CPUs have a set of built-in "instructions" in them. They define the various actions the CPU can take - things like taking in data from a keyboard, storing data in the computer, sending data to a display, etc.

The basic job of all processors is to execute various combinations of those simple instructions built into them. It only ever performs one of these instructions at a time, but modern computers can perform billions of instructions per second.

All actions you can make a computer do will be composed of various combinations of these built-in actions.

EXAMPLE: If you have a list of students in a computer file and you give the computer an instruction to put the list in alphabetical order, it is the CPU that performs the analysis and re-ordering of the list.

Peripheral: These are things that can be hooked up to a computer, including external devices. Peripherals include mice, keyboards, external drives, displays etc. Peripherals are often used to get data into a computer, or to receive data from the computer.

EXAMPLE: A printer is a peripheral.

Input: Input is data or information that is collected by a computer. This can take many forms. It may be information a user has typed into a form on the computer. It may be electronic signals sent to the computer by an attached device, like a mouse or a display screen that takes touch input. It may be a set of electronic data from another computer that is connected to the first one by wires.

EXAMPLE: A customer service agent at a retail store takes down your information and types it into her computer; that information is input for the computer to use.

Algorithm: A mathematics word that means a plan for solving a problem. Algorithms consist of a sequence of steps to solve a problem or perform an action. Computers use algorithms. An algorithm is a set of instructions that is used to get something done.

EXAMPLE: An algorithm for selecting the right kind of shirt might have the following steps:

```
1. Pick a shirt from your closet.
2. Put the shirt on.
3. Look at yourself in the mirror.
4. Decide whether you like the way you look in that shirt. If you like
how you look, leave the shirt on and go to step 6. If you do not like
how you look, take the shirt off and put it back in the closet where
you got it from.
5. Repeat steps 1 -5 until you have made a decision about each shirt
in the closet.
6. End this procedure.
```

Instruction: A command or set of commands entered into a computer that performs a certain operation. Instructions control a computer and tell it what to do.

EXAMPLE: You could make a computer draw a square by typing in instructions.

Program: Programs are written instructions, entered into the computer, that make it perform certain tasks.

Programs are the things on a computer that you interact with to get things done. You use a program of one sort or another for basically everything you do on your computer, whether that is checking the weather or looking up banking information. There are countless programs that people have created over the years to do countless different things.

EXAMPLE: "Paint" is a program on many computers that allows users to draw and color things.

Programmer: A computer programmer is someone who can create computer programs. Another term for programmer is developer.

A programmer can type exact commands and instructions in a computer to create many of the things we use computers for on a day-to-day basis.

EXAMPLE: Microsoft Word (a program mainly used to write documents) was created by programmers.

Programming Language: In order to understand the term programming language, you will need to understand the term language.

Languages are communication systems that allow you to transfer ideas in written and spoken words.

Programming languages are organized systems of words, phrases and symbols that let you create programs.

Programming languages are also called computer languages.

There are many different types of programming languages, each of which was created to fill a specific purpose. Usually a language is created in order to make the creation of certain types of computer programs easier.

EXAMPLE: Python is a popular computer language. This is how you would tell a computer to display the words “Hello, world!” on the screen, using the computer language Python:

```
print (“Hello, world!”)
```

Machine Language: A machine instruction is an instruction to your computer written in a form the CPU can understand - machine code or machine language.

The basic job of all processors is to execute various combinations of those simple instructions built into them. It only ever performs one of these instructions at a time, but modern computers can perform billions of instructions per second.

All actions you can make a computer do will be composed of various combinations of these built-in actions.

These built-in instructions are called machine instructions. Together, they are machine language.

Machine language is data that is composed of a series of 1s and 0s; computers are operated using 1s and 0s since it is very easy to make a machine that only has to differentiate between two different states.

When computers are manufactured, the CPU is made so it will obey certain instructions and perform exact actions when given those instructions. The machine instructions are available from the manufacturer of the computer.

EXAMPLE: Let's say "10010100 01101011 01011011 01010110" told the computer to "Delete the file called Vacation.doc." The "10010100 01101011 01011011 01010110" is a machine instruction.

It is difficult for people to read and write in machine language, since the instructions are just unique patterns of ones and zeroes.

Low-level language: A low-level language is a programming language that is at, or just above machine language in terms of readability - that is, it uses codes to represent specific machine language instructions, or different combinations of machine language instructions.

These codes are not the ones and zeroes of machine language; rather, they might look like this:

```
MOV AL, 61h
```

This might be codes that mean "store the amount 97 in a special location in the CPU for later use".

This is more readable than ones and zeros of machine language, but is still not very easy to work in.

Code: There are a couple of definitions for "code." The first is: what you type into a computer to make programs. Code is written in specialized computer languages. Coding means typing out instructions (using a particular computer language) to make a program that will make the computer perform certain actions.

EXAMPLE: You can write code that makes a computer game.

Code can also mean: A system where you use a symbol to represent another thing.

EXAMPLE: Airports are often referred to by three-letter codes - the Portland International Airport in Portland, Oregon, USA has the three-letter code PDX. So here, "PDX" is a code that represents the Portland International Airport.

Operating System: Abbreviated OS. An operating system is a special-purpose computer program that supports the computer's basic functions, such as scheduling tasks, running other computer programs, and controlling peripherals (external devices such as keyboards, mice and displays).

Most computer programs will require that an operating system already be installed on a computer before they can function on that computer.

Nearly all computers available today come with an operating system already installed when they are purchased. Computer manufacturers install the operating system before they sell a computer.

Some operating systems are free; others are available for a fee.

One of the most well-known and popular operating systems in the world is called Windows. It is created and sold by the technology company Microsoft.

Other popular operating systems are: OS X (created by the technology company Apple; it is used on their desktop computers and laptops); Linux (a family of free and for-fee operating systems; it is used on desktop computers and laptops); Android (owned by the technology company Google; it is used on mobile devices like smartphones) and iOS (created by Apple; it is used on their mobile devices like the iPhone and iPad).

EXAMPLE: Windows 10 is a popular operating system.

Network: A network is a system where two or more computers are connected to each other. The computers can be connected by a cable (wired) or connected wirelessly. Network is the word used to describe a link between things that are working together. Networks are used in many different ways with computers.

EXAMPLE: Information can be shared from computer to computer through the use of a network.

Internet: The Internet is two things: an interconnected network of many computers around the world, and a set of methods, or protocols, for transferring different types of data between those computers.

This is the basic definition of the internet. A detailed description follows.

A protocol is a formal description of how a certain type of information will be formatted and handled. Basically, it's an agreement that the various people who work with that type of information all adhere to. Protocols are usually described in written documents, and are very precise. They are usually created by experts in the applicable industry.

An example of a type of data where a protocol would be valuable is healthcare information. If various organizations in the healthcare industry were to transfer healthcare data back and forth between computers as they perform their work, it would be important that they all agree about things like the exact format of the information, how to keep private data safe, etc. All of that would be laid down in a written protocol. Several such protocols do exist in the healthcare industry.

The Internet is a network of connected computers, and there are lots of different types of data that can be sent back and forth between these computers - things like electronic messages, electronic documents, healthcare records, etc. One or more protocols have been created for each type of data that can be transferred around on the Internet.

EXAMPLE: A bank could devise a protocol for how to format and exchange financial data between its headquarters and its various branches, and then use their computers connected to the internet to actually exchange that data.

World Wide Web: Abbreviated WWW; usually referred to as "the Web". To understand what the World Wide Web is, you need to know about these other terms: web site, web page, web browser, and web server.

The World Wide Web (the "Web") is a collection of linked electronic documents, organized into groups called web sites.

The Web is accessed by connecting to the Internet. The computers involved in the operation of the Web are connected to the Internet,

A web site is composed of one or more individual web pages, where a "page" is an organized, separate document containing text, images, video and other elements. The electronic files that make up a web site are stored on specialized computers called web servers. These computers accept requests from other, remote computers for specific web pages, and deliver those files needed to make the web page display on the remote computer. The type of program you would use to view web pages is called a web browser. It is this program that would make the requests to the web server for the web site files.

EXAMPLE: There are web sites on the World Wide Web dedicated to the films of famous actors.

SMALL BASIC

Small Basic is a programming language broadly released by Microsoft in 2011. Small Basic includes an Integrated Development Environment (IDE – a tool in which one writes their code) and libraries (sets of pre-manufactured code for use). It can be used to write basic programs and games.

The .NET Framework is a collection of tools and pre-made software that helps software developers to make computer programs. It was created by Microsoft. It has several programming languages that it can work with. As a developer, you can write a program that uses one or more of these languages. The .NET Framework can take these programs and convert them down to instructions that will work on pretty much any computer that is compatible with this .NET Framework. This means you only have to write the program once, and not have to write variations of it for all the various types of computers you'd like to have run the program.

Small Basic is based on .NET and so familiarizing yourself with Small Basic makes it easier to learn other .NET programming languages, such as C#, in the future. This book is the perfect undercut for those interested in learning C# and other .NET technologies.

The purpose of Small Basic is to provide a programming language that is designed to make programming more approachable for newcomers. It is a great learning resource for beginners!

If you run into any trouble while going through this book, here are some tips:

1. Ensure you understand all the words and terms being used – clear up any you don't understand.
2. Ensure your code is written exactly as laid out here. A small error in the code, such as a typo, can ruin the whole program. Code must be exact for programs to run properly, so always meticulously check your code for errors.
3. Research online for solutions.
4. Contact The Tech Academy.

SECTION TWO
WHAT IS CODING?

Coding is computer programming. Computer programming is the act of creating computer programs, which are prepared sets of computer instructions designed to accomplish certain tasks. Programming consists of typing exact commands and instructions into a computer to create many of the things we use on computers on a day-to-day basis. To do computer programming, you must learn various programming languages and use these languages to create things on a computer that others can use.

EXAMPLE: The program on your computer entitled "calculator", which you can use to do math, is the result of computer programming.

Coding also refers to the creation of websites.

Another word for these programs is "software". This is because the actual computer (the physical machine) is called "hardware." Therefore, the programs that run on that machine are called "software."

The terms "coding" and "development" mean the same thing as programming. A software developer is a computer programmer; so is a coder.

Programming is a spectacular thing because it is one of the few skills that apply to virtually all industries. Yes, companies that create software definitely utilize coding the most - but if you think about it, most industries utilize technology (software, websites, databases, etc.) And so, coders are valuable assets for companies in any industry - construction, food service, retail, transportation, etc.

There are many, many programming languages, and technology is ever-changing. The whole thing can be quite overwhelming, but there are basics that apply across the vast landscape of technology.

In general, the instructions in computer programs are executed in order, from the top down.

FIVE ELEMENTS

There are five key elements to any computer program:

1. Entrance
2. Control/branching
3. Variables
4. Sub Program
5. Exit

Let's take a look at each of these.

ENTRANCE

1. Entrance:

A computer is a simple machine when you get down to it. It can only do one thing at a time, and it performs a computer program's instructions in the exact order in which the computer programmer puts them. It can only execute (perform, or run) an instruction if it is directed to.

This means that any computer program has to have a clearly marked "first instruction". This is the first task that the computer will perform when the computer program is started. From that point forward, each instruction in the program will direct the computer what instruction to perform next after it performs the current instruction.

There are different ways to specify the entrance point, depending on which computer programming language is being used - but every computer program has a defined entrance point.

CONTROL/BRANCHING

2. Control/Branching

Computers are often used to automate actions that would otherwise be performed by people. One of the most common things a person will be asked to do in performing a job is to assess the condition of a thing and, based on the condition of that thing, choose between two or more possible courses of action. In other words, they will have to make a decision. An example would be the activity of "a teacher grading a stack of papers":

- Take the next student paper from the top of the stack.
- Grade the paper.
- Write the grade on the paper.
- If the grade is 70% or higher, put the paper in a "Passed" stack.
- If the grade is below 70%, put the paper in a "Failed" stack.

You can see that there are two possible "paths" here. A path is: "a possible course of action arising from a decision". Think of it as what happens when you come to a fork in the road. You have to decide on a course of action - which road do you take?

All but the simplest of computer programs will need to do the same thing. That is, they will have to check the condition of a piece of data, and, based on the condition of that data, they will have to execute different sets of computer instructions.

In order to do this, the program will make use of special computer instructions called "control" instructions. These are just instructions that tell the computer what to look at in making a decision, and then tell the computer what to do for each possible decision. The most fundamental control statement for a computer is "if". It is used like this:

IF [condition to check checked] THEN [branch of computer instructions to execute]

Here, the "IF" is the control statement; the "THEN" is the branching instruction that points to the path of the program to execute if the control statement is true.

VARIABLES

3. Variables

A variable is a piece of data that a computer program uses to keep track of values that can change as the program is executed. This might be something like "the grade of the student paper that was just graded," or "the color of paint to use for the next car on the assembly line."

Variables are a vital part of any computer program, because they make it so a computer program can be used for more than a single, pre-determined set of values. You can imagine that if "the color of paint to use for the next car on the assembly line" was only ever able to be "blue," the computer program using that data wouldn't be very useful. It would make a lot more sense to make it so the computer program could change that value for each car that was going to be painted.

When you are writing variables in a computer program, they usually are written in a manner like this:

[name of the variable] = [value of the variable]

For example, you might have something like this:

color = "red"

Here, the variable is named "color", and the value of that variable has been set to "red." In other words, the variable named "color" is now "equal" to the word "red."

Let's look at the example of "a teacher grading a stack of papers". Here, we could have a variable called "Paper Grade" that changed each time the teacher graded a paper. You could also have variables for the total number of questions on the paper ("Total Questions"), for the number of questions the student answered correctly

("Correct Questions"), and for the grade of the paper.

The written description from above:

- Take the next student paper from the top of the "To Be Graded" stack.
- Grade the paper.
- Write the grade on the paper.
- If the grade is 70% or higher, put the paper in a "Passed" stack.
- If the grade is below 70%, put the paper in a "Failed" stack.

In computer language, the procedure might look something like this:

1. Retrieve next Paper
2. Set Total Questions = [total questions in current Paper]
3. Grade paper
4. Set Correct Questions = [number of questions answered correctly]
5. Set Paper Grade = [Correct Questions/Total Questions]
6. If (Paper Grade >= 70%) then Paper Status = "passed"
7. If (Paper Grade < 70%) then Paper Status = "failed"

This is a simple computer program.

Each time the computer runs this program, it could have different values for each of the variables in the program, depending on how many questions the paper being graded has, and how many of those questions the student answered correctly.

For example, let's say the paper has 100 questions, and the student answers 82 of them correctly. After the program is run, the result would be the following:

Total Questions: 100
Correct Questions: 82
Paper Grade: 82%
Paper Status: "passed"

Another example: Let's say the paper has 50 questions, and the student answers 30 of them correctly. After the program is run, the result would be the following:

Total Questions: 50
Correct Questions: 30
Paper Grade: 60%
Paper Status: "failed"

To clarify the need for variables: Let's say that, at the time this computer program was being created, all papers at the school had 100 questions, and the teachers told the programmer to make it so that the number of questions was always assumed to be 100. In that case, the programmer wouldn't use a variable called "Total Questions." Instead, he could make the program look like this:

1. Retrieve next Paper
2. Grade paper
3. Set Correct Questions = [number of questions answered correctly]
4. Set Paper Grade = [Correct Questions/100]
5. If (Paper Grade >= 70%) then Paper Status = "passed"
6. If (Paper Grade < 70%) then Paper Status = "failed"

Notice that on line 4 of the program, the programmer set the number of questions to 100.

Now, let's say that the school introduces the concept of "quizzes," which are smaller papers with only 20 questions. Now, if the paper being handled by the computer program is a quiz, the grade will no longer be accurate - even if a student got all 20 questions correct, he/she would only get a grade of 20% (20/100).

A good programmer will analyze the need that the program is meant to resolve, then build the program so that it can handle changing aspects of that need over time.

Another valuable control statement is a loop. This is where part of the program is executed over and over, until a certain condition is met.

In real world terms, an example might be "grade papers, one at a time, until all the papers have been graded," or "make five copies of this document."

In a computer program, a loop would look something like this:

- [start loop]
  - Perform action
  - If [end condition has been met] then [exit the loop]
  - If [end condition has not been met] then [repeat the loop]
- [end loop]

The program we looked at that grades papers could be set up as a loop. The instructions would be laid out like this:

- [start loop]
  - Take the next student paper from the top of the "To Be Graded" stack.
  - Grade the paper.
  - Write the grade on the paper.
  - If the grade is 70% or higher, put the paper in a "Passed" stack.

  - If the grade is below 70%, put the paper in a "Failed" stack.
  - If there are no more papers in the "To Be Graded" stack, exit the loop
  - If there are more papers in the "To Be Graded" stack, repeat the loop
- [end loop]

Often, loops make use of a special variable called a "counter." The counter keeps track of how many times the loop has been executed. This can be used to make sure the loop is only executed when needed.

Let's add a counter to the grading program we're looking at, as well as two new variables: "Total Papers"will be used to hold the value "how many papers are need to be graded" and "Counter" will be used to hold the value "how many times has the loop been executed."

1. Set Total Papers = [total papers to be graded]
2. Set Counter = 0
3. If (Counter < Total Papers)
    a. Retrieve next Paper
    b. Set Total Questions = [total questions in current Paper]
    c. Grade paper
    d. Set Correct Questions = [number of questions answered correctly]
    e. Set Paper Grade = [Correct Questions/Total Questions]
    f. If (Paper Grade >= 70%) then Paper Status = "passed"
    g. If (Paper Grade < 70%) then Paper Status = "failed"
    h. Counter = Counter + 1
    i. Go to step 3
4. [Continue on with the rest of the program]

Here, the loop is found in step 3.

Let's break down what each step is doing here:

Step 1: Count how many papers are in the "to be graded" stack and set the value of the "Total Papers" variable to that number.
Step 2: Create a variable called "Counter" and set it to the value zero. This variable will be used to keep track of how many papers are graded.
Step 3: Use the control statement "if" to see if we should execute a loop.
Step 3a - 3g: Grade the paper; this has been covered above.
Step 3h: Since we have now graded a paper, add one to our Counter variable.
Step 3i: Go to the top of the loop, where we check to see if we need to execute the loop all over again.

Let's see what would happen if we used this program to grade two papers. Let's say that the papers look like this:

Paper 1:
Total questions on the paper: 100
Total questions that were answered correctly: 95

Paper 2:
Total questions on the paper: 20
Total questions that were answered correctly: 10

If we analyze what happens when the program is executed by the computer, it would look like this:

Total Papers = 2
Counter = 0
0 is less than 2, so loop will be executed
Paper 1 retrieved
Total Questions = 100
Paper 1 graded
Correct Questions = 95
Paper Grade = 95%
Paper Status = "passed"
Counter = 1
1 is less than 2, so loop will be executed
Paper 2 retrieved
Total Questions = 20
Paper 1 graded
Correct Questions = 10
Paper Grade = 50%
Paper Status = "failed"
Counter = 2
2 is not less than 2, so loop will not be executed
[Continue on with the rest of the program]

SUB PROGRAMS

4. Sub Programs

As covered above, computer programs are generally executed in order, from the start point to the end point. This is called the “path of execution.”

The main series of instructions in a program is called the "main program.”

It is sometimes valuable to create another program that can be used by the main program as needed. This is called a sub program. It is no different from any other program - it is made up of the same elements (entrance point, variables, control & branching statements and exit point). However, a sub program isn't used all by itself.

Instead, the main program can execute the sub program as needed. Here, the main program stops executing, and the sub program starts executing. When the sub program is done executing, the main program continues on where it left off.

This is called "calling" the sub program - that is, the main program calls the sub program, the sub program starts and stops, and the main program continues on where it left off before calling the sub program.

This is useful in creating programs because the computer programmer doesn't have to enter the instructions of the sub program over and over - you only type them in once, and then when you need that sub program to be called by the main program, you only have to type in one instruction - the instruction to call the sub program. This lets you reuse the instructions you entered in for the sub program, rather than rewriting them.

EXIT

5. Exit:

Every program must have an instruction that tells the computer that the program is no longer running. Much like the Entrance, the exact instruction for this varies based on the computer language used, but all computer languages will have this type of instruction.

Small Basic is a wonderful tool to teach you the 5 key elements of a computer program.

End of Section Challenges

At the end of some sections, we will have an "END OF SECTION CHALLENGE." At times you will also be instructed to figure out new things on your own. These are opportunities for you to put together all that you've studied in that section thus far and more. Working software developers are often assigned projects and tasks they've never done before. A key element of the job is researching solutions online and therefore, some of these challenges will instruct you to do something that we haven't taught you yet. This is intentional so that you gain experience in locating new data online and figuring out things on your own. In the words of more than one software developer: "I get paid to Google things!"

Installation

Here is your first task:

Go to http://smallbasic.com/ and download Small Basic. Then, install it on your computer, using all default settings.

SECTION THREE
HELLO WORLD

Now that Small Basic is installed on your machine:

Launch SmallBasic.

You should see something similar to the following:

This is the IDE (Integrated Development Environment) that you will be using to write your code as you create computer programs.

The white area where you will type your code is called the "Editor."

The top bar, where such options as New, Open and Save are listed, is called the "Toolbar."

To write code, you simply type text inside the Editor.

A very common first program that people write when starting out with a programming language is to have the computer display the words: “Hello World.”

Type the following inside the Editor:

```
TextWindow.WriteLine("Hello World!")
```

You've written your first program using SmallBasic. Now, there are two ways to run the program:

1. Click the Run button on the Toolbar, or
2. Press F5 on your keyboard.

Run your program.

If you have created the program correctly, you should see a console window that looks like this:

If you didn't get that result, check your work and try again. If you did get that result, good job!

It is wise to save your code regularly. You don't want your computer to shut off after you've spent hours writing out code – that will result in losing all your hard work. You can save your code in two ways:

1. Click Save on the Toolbar, or
2. While holding down the Ctrl key on the keyboard, press S and then release both keys.

Save your program. Give it any filename you like.

SECTION FOUR
ANALYZING THE PROGRAM

A statement is an instruction given to a computer. Each line of code you write is a statement. Your Small Basic programs will usually be composed of a series of statements.

When you execute a Small Basic program, the computer reads and executes the first statement. After executing the first statement, it moves onto the next statement and executes that, etc.

In our Hello World program, we only wrote one statement. The statement instructed the computer to display the text "Hello World!"

Programming languages each have their own syntax. These are the required rules when writing code in a particular language. Syntax is like grammar. Violation of syntax will result in your code not running properly. Let's analyze the syntax of the code you wrote: TextWindow.WriteLine("Hello World!")

Here are all the elements within our code:

1. TextWindow
2. WriteLine
3. Hello World!
4. . (a period)
5. () (parentheses)
6. "" (quotation marks)

Each of the above points communicate an exact thing to your computer.

TextWindow is an object. There are many objects you can use in Small Basic and TextWindow is one of them. This is what the text window looks like:

C:\Users\User\AppData\Local\Temp\tmp4BD6.tmp.exe
Hello World!
Press any key to continue...

This is also called the Console and is where the result of the program is displayed.

In Small Basic, we are able to perform actions on objects. These actions are called operations. The operation we performed earlier on the TextWindow object was “WriteLine.” There are many other operations that can be performed in Small Basic.

The “Hello World!” is a parameter (data given to an operation for use as the operation is performed) for our WriteLine operation. Operations can either accept one or more parameters or none at all.

Parentheses, quotation marks and periods all perform various functions when writing code and are part of its syntax. For example: In Small Basic, to print text you must type the desired text within quotation marks (“”).

SECTION FIVE
EXPANDING THE PROGRAM

Now we will perform another operation on the TextWindow object. Write and execute the following code:

Write the following code in the Editor, above TextWindow.WriteLine("Hello World"):
TextWindow.BackgroundColor = "White"
TextWindow.ForegroundColor = "Blue"

We have used the operations BackgroundColor and ForegroundColor on the object TextWindow. We have given the operations the parameters "White" and "Blue." You can play around with this and change the parameter to other colors such as yellow, red, green, etc.

Change the foreground color.
Change the background color.

As a note, you can find the full list of colors for Small Basic here:

https://blogs.msdn.microsoft.com/smallbasic/2015/06/20/the-hex-colors-in-small-basic/

These operations (unlike the WriteLine operation) did not need parentheses and didn't take any inputs. We used an equal sign to assign the values (in these cases, colors).

The ForegroundColor and BackgroundColor are properties of the object (TextWindow).

Change the foreground color again. This time, delete the quotation marks (" ") around the value and attempt running your program.

You will receive an error message. This is an example of a syntax error. Something as simple as leaving out quotation marks can cause a program not to run.

Fix the error.

As we just covered, each color is a parameter (which is, again, the data given to an operation for use as the operation is performed).

As we discussed earlier, a variable is a symbol used to represent an unknown quantity or a quantity that may change. In computers, a variable is used to store data for later use as the program executes.

Computers often have to keep track of various pieces of information. These can be things like the name of a computer user, the color of the background shown on the computer screen, an order number for something a user ordered from a company, etc.

The computer usually gives each of these pieces of data a NAME and a VALUE. The NAME is used to identify the exact piece of data, and the VALUE is used to show the actual data we need to keep track of.

These things the computer is keeping track of are usually called "variables". This is because the VALUE part of it can change when you tell the computer to change it. The fact that the value can vary is why it's called a "variable" – its value is not permanent or constant.

Usually the "=" symbol is used to set the VALUE of a variable.

When the "=" symbol is used to set the value of a variable, it is usually used like this:
[NAME of the variable] = [VALUE that is being assigned to that variable]

EXAMPLE: fabricColor = "blue".

Here, there is a piece of data that the computer is keeping track of that has been given the name "fabricColor". By using the "=" symbol, we can set the value of the piece of data called "fabricColor". In this case, we are setting that value to the series of letters "blue".

END OF SECTION CHALLENGE

Write a program that contains the following elements:

-A background color,
-A foreground color,
-The TextWindow.Pause() operation, and
-The WriteLine operation.

Note: You are being asked to use the TextWindow.Pause() operation which is something you haven't learned in this book. As we mentioned earlier, you will occasionally be tasked with performing actions you haven't been taught yet. This is intentional and is a vital component of the learning process. Remember to research online for solutions and data as needed.

SECTION SIX
MORE VARIABLES

Let's make it so the program can store and print variables.

Write and execute the following code:

```
TextWindow.Write("What is your favorite food?: ")
food = TextWindow.Read()
TextWindow.WriteLine("Your favorite food is " + food + "! Yummy!")
TextWindow.Write("Which city would you most like to visit?: ")
city = TextWindow.Read()
TextWindow.WriteLine(city + " sounds like a great place to visit! Don't forget to bring
your computer with you!")
```

Read() in your above code is an operation that instructs the computer to stand by for the user to type something and then press the Enter/Return key. After the user types in data and hits Enter/Return, the computer takes what they typed and returns it to the program.

As covered earlier, a variable is a place where values are stored for later use. In your code, food and city are variables. The text the user types in response to food and city are stored in variables. The variable "food" was used to store the user's favorite food, while the variable "city" was used to store the city that the user wished to visit.

When naming a variable, it is recommended that you use a name that describes the variable. For example: user_address = TextWindow.Read() would be a good name for a variable that stores a user's home address, whereas giraffe = TextWindow.Read() would not be a good name for storing user address data.

END OF SECTION CHALLENGE

Write a program that contains the following elements:
-The TextWindow.Write operation,
-The TextWindow.Read operation, and
-The CursorTop property (note: a property is an attribute of an object).

SECTION SEVEN
MATH AND NUMBERS

You can also store and utilize numbers in variables and perform mathematical equations.

Write and execute the following code:

```
First_number = 5
Second_number = 10
Third_number = 15
Fourth_number = 20
Fifth_number = 50
Sixth_number = 16
TextWindow.WriteLine(Second_number + Third_number)
```

We just added 10 and 15 together.

The variable numbers have been assigned various values, as follows:

- You assigned the variable First_number the value 5
- You assigned the variable Second_number the value 10
- You assigned the variable Third_number the value 15
- You assigned the variable Fourth_number the value 20
- You assigned the variable Fifth_number the value 50
- You assigned the variable Sixth_number the value 16

When we used "text" as a parameter earlier, we were required to surround the text with quotation marks, but with numeric parameters, quotation marks are unnecessary.

You can also perform subtraction. Add the following code beneath your existing code and execute it:

```
TextWindow.WriteLine(25 - First_number)
```

You can multiply numbers. Add the following code beneath your existing code and execute it:

```
TextWindow.WriteLine(20 * Fourth_number)
```

You can divide numbers as well. Add the following code beneath your existing code and execute it:

```
TextWindow.WriteLine(400 / Fifth_number)
```

We can also get the square root of a number. Add the following code beneath your existing code and execute it:

```
TextWindow.WriteLine(Math.SquareRoot (Sixth_number))
```

To explain the code you just wrote: the "Math" code you used here is an example of a library. In computer programming, a "library" is a pre-made package of computer code. Libraries are useful in computer programming because it means the programmer doesn't have to write the code to do the functions that the library provides, he or she can just use the pre-made library.

"Math" is a library that's built into Small Basic. SquareRoot is an operation available from the Math library.

Using the Math library, you can also round numbers. Add the following code beneath your existing code and execute it:

```
TextWindow.WriteLine(Math.Round(5.6))
```

Feel free to play around with your variables and different math operations.

Another interesting thing you can do with Small Basic is convert temperature from Fahrenheit to Celsius.

The way you convert Fahrenheit to Celsius is: Fahrenheit temperature subtracted by 32, multiplied by 5/9ths. Or written as an equation:
$T_{(°C)} = (T_{(°F)} - 32) \times 5/9$

Add the following code beneath your existing code and execute it:

```
TextWindow.Write("What is temperature in Fahrenheit?: ")
Fahrenheit = TextWindow.ReadNumber()
Celsius = (Fahrenheit - 32) * 5/9
TextWindow.WriteLine("The temperature in Fahrenheit converted to Celsius is: " +
Celsius)
```

We can also write a short program that randomly provides the user with a number.

Write and execute the following code:

```
TextWindow.WriteLine(Math.GetRandomNumber(100))
```

END OF SECTION CHALLENGE

Write a program that includes the following:

-The TextWindow.Title property,
-Assigning a value to a variable,
-The TextWindow.WriteLine operation, and
-The TextWindow.Top property.

SECTION EIGHT
CONDITIONAL STATEMENTS

A condition is something that other things depend on. In math, a condition is something that is required for something else to be true. Conditions are points that are necessary to be present for other points to be present. If you say something is "conditional", that means it relies on the state of another thing.

EXAMPLE: The statement "Electricity is allowed to flow through this part of the computer if you type 1" could be a condition. Or say you have a word problem like this: "Come up with two digits that, when added together, equal six – but the digits 2 and 4 are never to be used to get the answer." Here, the part that tells you that you can't use the numbers 2 or 4 in your answer is a condition.

A conditional statement takes place when you tell the computer: depending upon ___, do ___. An "If Statement" is a type of conditional statement that means: if this, then that.

A branch is a point of decision. Branches are a fundamental element of how we make computers do useful work. A branch instruction tells the computer to go to somewhere other than the primary series of instructions and instead execute an alternate series of instructions; usually based on some decision the computer has to make. It is a statement written in the program's code to make the computer shift from one area to another.

EXAMPLE: If you are using a computer program to order food from a restaurant, and the restaurant has a different procedure for ordering if you want the food to be delivered instead of being set aside for you to pick up, there will be a branch in the computer program where the user will be prompted as to whether their order is for pickup or delivery. In this case, the computer will have two series of steps it will perform. The branch instruction in the computer program will execute one or the other of these series, depending on the user's response.

In order to tell the computer how to analyze conditional statements, you'll make use of comparison instructions, such as the < and > symbols.

Write and execute the following code:

```
If (5 < 10) Then
  TextWindow.WriteLine("Five is less than 10.")
EndIf
```

The EndIf statement tells the computer that we are done with that operation.

END OF SECTION CHALLENGE

Write and execute your own conditional statement.

SECTION NINE
MORE CONDITIONAL STATEMENTS

Now let's try using an ElseIf Statement, which is basically a second If Statement and gives us another option to choose from. We will also use an Else Statement that tells the computer, "Otherwise, do ___." You'll get a better idea of this through trying it out.

Write and execute the following code:

```
start:
TextWindow.Write("Are you a vegan?: ")
Vegan = TextWindow.Read()
If Vegan = "Yes" Then
  TextWindow.WriteLine("I know, you've told me already. Several times...")
ElseIf Vegan = "No" Then
  TextWindow.WriteLine("Looks like meat is back on the menu!")
Else
  TextWindow.WriteLine("Please enter Yes or No.")
  Goto start
EndIf
```

We also added a couple new things to your code above:

1. Start:. This is called a label. It's similar to a bookmark within your program. In this case, the start label defines the beginning of our code and gave us a place to return to in our program, and
2. Goto: This is an instruction which makes the program go to an exact place in the series of instructions that make up the program. "Goto" statements utilize labels and redirect the program to a label.

Here is another comparison instruction:

>= (greater-than sign followed by equal sign). This symbol is used to show that a comparison should be made. Specifically, this "greater-than or equal" symbol is basically an instruction to check whether the data on the left side of the symbol is more than or equal in amount or quantity than the data on the right side. The answer to this comparison is an answer of "true" or "false".

EXAMPLE: 6 >= 6. This means "check whether 6 is greater than or equal to 6". The answer is "true".

Now let's create a program that can tell the difference between a.m. and p.m. Write and execute the following code:

```
If (Clock.Hour < 12) Then
 TextWindow.WriteLine("It is a.m.")
ElseIf (Clock.Hour >= 12) Then
 TextWindow.WriteLine("It is p.m.")
EndIf
```

Clock.Hour is a built-in instruction in SmallBasic that gives the time on your computer; we used that to check the time. There is also another way you can write your code:

Write and execute the following code:

```
If (Clock.Hour < 12) Then
 TextWindow.WriteLine("It is a.m.")
 Else
  TextWindow.WriteLine("It is p.m.")
EndIf
```

As you can see, the code is sometimes automatically indented for you. This is so that the code is sectioned off and you can easily read through it. In Small Basic, this indentation isn't necessary and the program will run whether or not the code is indented.

Now let's use some of what we've learned so far (and learn some more) to build a program that will round numbers and tell us whether or not the numbers are odd or even.

In math, a "remainder" is the number left over after a division operation. Math.Remainder is an operation in Small Basic that divides the first number by the second and returns (gives back) the remainder. E.g. All even numbers will have a 0 remainder when divided by 2 (nothing left over – they divide evenly).

Write and execute the following code:

```
TextWindow.Write("Type a number that includes a decimal: ")
Number = TextWindow.ReadNumber()
TextWindow.Write("Now we will round your number! ...")
TextWindow.Write("Your rounded number is: " + Math.Round(Number) + ".")
Remainder = Math.Remainder(Math.Round(Number), 2)
If (Remainder = 0) Then
 TextWindow.WriteLine(" This number is even!")
 Else
  TextWindow.WriteLine(" This is an odd number!")
EndIf
```

Did you notice how the text all just blurted out? Let's add a delay so that one sentence displays at a time. To do so we use the Program.Delay() operation. Within the parentheses after "Delay", you enter how many milliseconds you want to wait before the program continues.

Write and execute the following code:

```
TextWindow.Write("Type a number that includes a decimal: ")
Number = TextWindow.ReadNumber()
Program.Delay(1000)
TextWindow.Write("Now we will round your number! ...")
Program.Delay(1000)
TextWindow.Write("Your rounded number is: " + Math.Round(Number) + ".")
Program.Delay(1000)
Remainder = Math.Remainder(Math.Round(Number), 2)
If (Remainder = 0) Then
 TextWindow.WriteLine(" This number is even!")
 Program.Delay(1000)
 Else
  TextWindow.WriteLine(" This is an odd number!")
  Program.Delay(1000)
EndIf
```

In our last program, the If Statement and the Else Statement are control statements while the code that is executed in response to those control statements are the branches.

In our last program, the first branch is:

```
TextWindow.WriteLine(" This number is even!")
Program.Delay(1000)
```

And the second branch is:

```
TextWindow.WriteLine(" This is an odd number!")
Program.Delay(1000)
```

<u>END OF SECTION CHALLENGE</u>

Write a program that includes the following:

-If statement,
-ElseIf statement,
-Else statement,
-Program.delay,

-Math.Remainder, and
-Math.Ceiling(number).

SECTION TEN
LOOPS

As we covered earlier, a loop is something that connects back to the beginning point. In computers, a loop is a sequence of instructions that are continually repeated until an exact condition is achieved.

Usually a loop will occur when a certain set of actions are performed by a computer program. The program would then check to see if it has reached the condition required for completion. If not, it starts over and repeats the set of actions. If so, it exits the loop and moves on to the next consecutive instruction in the computer program.

EXAMPLE: You tell the computer to search through a list of paint colors until the color "red" is found.

The list that the computer will search is this:

Blue
Yellow
Red
Orange
White

A loop is written into the computer and looks something like this:

Step 1: Get next consecutive item in the list.
Step 2: Check whether the item equals "Red".
Step 3: If the item equals "Red", exit this loop.
Step 4: If the item is not equal to "Red", loop back to step 1.

When this loop is executed, it will go like this:
Step 1: Acquired "Blue"
Step 2: Checked if "Blue" equal to "Red"
Step 3: Item not equal to "Red". Did not exit the loop.
Step 4: Item not equal to "Red". Looped back to Step 1.
Step 1: Acquired "Yellow"
Step 2: Checked if "Yellow" equal to "Red"
Step 3: Item not equal to "Red". Did not exit the loop.
Step 4: Item not equal to "Red". Looped back to Step 1.
Step 1: Acquired "Red"
Step 2: Checked if "Red" equal to "Red"
Step 3: Item equal to "Red". Exited the loop.

A couple of important types of loops are "While Loops" and "For Loops."

A "While Loop" is basically a repeating "if statement." Meaning, you are telling the computer to execute certain code repeatedly *while* a particular condition is present. E.g. While hungry, eat.

Write and execute the following code in the text Editor:

```
Amount = 1
While (Amount < 1025)
 TextWindow.WriteLine(Amount)
 Amount = Amount * 2
EndWhile
```

In this program we are telling the program that "As long as the Amount is less than 1025, multiply the Amount by 2."

An important aspect of how loops work is the concept of an iteration.

To iterate means to say or do something again; to repeat something. An iteration is the act of repeating. Iteration means to go through a defined series of actions, repeating a certain number of times. Usually this defined series of actions is repeated a certain number of times, or until a condition is met.

EXAMPLE: Computer programs are usually created in iterations: Coming up with a basic working version, reviewing the program for mistakes to correct and improvements to make, doing that work, and repeating. When the program works acceptably, this process starts.

A "For Loop" is used to repeat a section of code a number of times. For Loops are used when the number of iterations are known. Here's an example: for each student in the class (25), provide a grade.

Write and execute the following for loop:

```
For B = 1 To 10
 TextWindow.WriteLine(B)
EndFor
```

In our code, we assign the values 1 through 10 to the variable B, one at a time, as the loop is executed. An integer is a whole number (such as 3 or 5). An increment is a distinct increase in amount. Incrementing is to distinctly increase a number. "1 To 10" above was incrementing an integer. But since we assigned a variable ("B"), we were technically "incrementing a variable." And so, we utilized a For Loop to increment a variable.

If we create a loop and don't close the loop, the code will continue on forever. Here's an example:

Write and execute the following code:

```
Begin:
A = 50
If A > 25 Then
 TextWindow.WriteLine("50 is more than 25!")
 Goto Begin
EndIf
```

You will see that when this program is executed, the computer just continues to print "50 is more than 25!" to the screen until you close the window. This is because the condition statement in your loop ("If A > 25") is always true, so the loop always returns to the beginning and does another iteration. This is called an "infinite loop"; under certain circumstances this can lock up a computer and require the shutdown and restart of the computer in order to stop the loop.

To close the loop in our example, you would simply get rid of the "Begin:" label and the "Goto" statement.

Now, let's make a program – using a For Loop – that counts out only even numbers up to 30.

Write and execute the following code:

```
For B = 2 To 30 Step 2
 TextWindow.WriteLine(B)
EndFor
```

"Step" in your code counts up or down depending on the values you assign. So now, let's reverse the countdown and use only odd numbers!

Write and execute the following code:

```
For B = 29 To 1 Step -2
 TextWindow.WriteLine(B)
EndFor
```

It's interesting to note that every Loop can be translated into a Conditional Statement. For example, we can rewrite our last For Loop as follows:

Write and execute the following code:

```
B = 29
Start:
TextWindow.WriteLine(B)
B = B - 2
If (0 < B) Then
  Goto Start
EndIf
```

Actually, fun fact: every time you write a While Loop in your code, the computer automatically converts it to an If Statement with one or more Goto Statements. This is done behind the scenes; you won't see the actual instructions you typed in the editor change.

Let's do another loop that will find out the larger of two numbers.

Write and execute the following code:

```
TextWindow.Write("Type in a number: ")
First_Number = TextWindow.ReadNumber()
TextWindow.Write("Type in another number: ")
Second_Number = TextWindow.ReadNumber()
If (First_Number > Second_Number) Then
  Larger = First_Number
  Else
    Larger = Second_Number
EndIf
TextWindow.WriteLine("The larger number is: " + Larger)
```

END OF SECTION CHALLENGE 1

Write a program that includes the following:

-A For Loop, and
-A While Loop.

END OF SECTION CHALLENGE 2

Write a program that includes the following:

-Create a loop that counts numbers backwards, one number at a time, starting at 100 down to 1, that also includes Program.Delay(100).

SECTION ELEVEN
GRAPHICS WINDOW

You can customize certain aspects of the Text Window and how it displays. We touched upon this earlier with foreground color and background color.

There is also a graphics window. Graphics are pictures displayed on a computer. Graphics are art created on a computer by a person.

Like the Text Window that displays text, Small Basic also has a Graphics Window for graphics.

Enter and execute the following code:

```
GraphicsWindow.Show()
```

Small Basic Graphics Window

That's what the window looks like. Now, to customize the Graphics Window, there are some things you can do.

Write and execute the following code:

```
GraphicsWindow.Height = 500
GraphicsWindow.Width = 700
GraphicsWindow.BackgroundColor = "Silver"
GraphicsWindow.Title = "The Graphics Window!"
GraphicsWindow.Show()
```

One of the cool things about the Graphics Window is the ability to draw lines.

Write and execute the following code:

```
GraphicsWindow.DrawLine(10,10,200,10)
GraphicsWindow.DrawLine(10,10,10,200)
GraphicsWindow.DrawLine(10,200,200,200)
GraphicsWindow.DrawLine(200,10,200,200)
```

Each line of code drew one side of the square. The X Coordinate refers to how far left to right (horizontally) something extends on a grid or a map. The Y Coordinate refers to how far top to bottom (vertically) something extends. Here's how each number in each line of code laid this out:

- The first number tells the computer how far left or right the line will be started (called the X Coordinate).
- The second number tells us where the line starts – up and down – (called the Y Coordinate).
- The third number tells the computer where the bottom of the line ends right to left.
- The fourth number tells the computer where the bottom of the line (up and down) ends up.

Let's try a challenge now. Write and execute the following code:

```
Draw an X shape using GraphicsWindow.DrawLine.
```

We can also change the color and thickness of the line.

Write and execute the following code:

```
GraphicsWindow.Height = 500
GraphicsWindow.Width = 500
GraphicsWindow.BackgroundColor = "Silver"
GraphicsWindow.Title = "The Colored Square!"
GraphicsWindow.DrawLine(10,10,450,10)
GraphicsWindow.PenWidth = 10
GraphicsWindow.PenColor = "Red"
GraphicsWindow.DrawLine(10,10,10,450)
GraphicsWindow.PenWidth = 20
GraphicsWindow.PenColor = "Blue"
GraphicsWindow.DrawLine(10,450,450,450)
GraphicsWindow.PenWidth = 30
GraphicsWindow.PenColor = "Yellow"
GraphicsWindow.DrawLine(450,10,450,450)
GraphicsWindow.PenWidth = 40
GraphicsWindow.PenColor = "Green"
```

We can also utilize a Loop with the Graphic Box.

Write and execute the following code:

```
GraphicsWindow.Title = "Growing Lines!"
GraphicsWindow.Height = 500
GraphicsWindow.Width = 500
GraphicsWindow.PenColor = "Red"
GraphicsWindow.BackgroundColor = "Blue"
For A = 1 To 15
  GraphicsWindow.PenWidth = A
  GraphicsWindow.DrawLine(20, A * 20, 400, A * 20)
EndFor
```

As you can see, we used a For Loop to gradually increase the thickness of the lines.

We can also draw pixels in the Graphics Window.

Write and execute the following code:

```
GraphicsWindow.SetPixel(20, 20, "Black")
```

If you can see it, there's a tiny black dot on the screen. The numbers give the X and Y coordinate for the pixel.

And in case you were wondering, we can also add text to the Graphics Window.

Write and execute the following code:

```
GraphicsWindow.DrawBoundText(70, 70, 150, "John")
GraphicsWindow.DrawBoundText(120, 70, 150, "Sally")
GraphicsWindow.DrawBoundText(180, 70, 150, "Bill")
GraphicsWindow.DrawBoundText(250, 70, 150, "Jessica")
GraphicsWindow.DrawBoundText(70, 120, 150, "John")
GraphicsWindow.DrawBoundText(120, 120, 150, "Sally")
GraphicsWindow.DrawBoundText(180, 120, 150, "Bill")
GraphicsWindow.DrawBoundText(250, 120, 150, "Jessica")
```

The first number gives the X Coordinate, the second number the Y Coordinate and the third number the size of the font.

END OF SECTION CHALLENGE

Write a program that includes the following:

-GraphicsWindow.Height,
-GraphicsWindow.Width,
-GraphicsWindow.DrawLine,
-GraphicsWindow.PenWidth,
-GraphicsWindow.PenColor,
-GraphicsWindow.SetPixel,
-GraphicsWindow.DrawBoundText with multiple font sizes, and
-GraphicsWindow.FontItalic.

SECTION TWELVE
SHAPES

We can also paint and create shapes in the Graphics Window.

Write and execute the following code:

```
GraphicsWindow.BrushColor = "Green"
GraphicsWindow.FillTriangle(300,150,150,300,450,300)
```

For a triangle we need six numbers. The first two indicate where the top of the triangle is placed (left to right, up to down). The second two indicate the left-hand corner and the third set indicates the right-hand corner.

You can also draw and paint: squares, rectangles and ellipses (ovals). To draw a circle, you would use the eclipse operation.

Write and execute the following code:

```
GraphicsWindow.Width = 300
GraphicsWindow.Height = 300
GraphicsWindow.BackgroundColor = "Black"
GraphicsWindow.PenColor = "Yellow"
GraphicsWindow.PenWidth = 20
GraphicsWindow.DrawEllipse(50, 50, 200, 200)
```

If you want to fill in the circle so that it looks like a sun, simply change your code.

Write and execute the following code:

```
GraphicsWindow.Width = 300
GraphicsWindow.Height = 300
GraphicsWindow.BackgroundColor = "Black"
GraphicsWindow.BrushColor = "Yellow"
GraphicsWindow.FillEllipse(50, 50, 200, 200)
```

Now let's make a circle using variables.

Write and execute the following code:

```
A = 20
B = 50
GraphicsWindow.FillEllipse(A, B, 350, 350)
```

You can also animate shapes and move them around.

Write and execute the following code:

```
Triangle = Shapes.AddTriangle(50, 100, 100, 50, 150, 100)
Program.Delay(1000)
Shapes.Animate(Triangle, 200, 200, 1000)
```

The first thing we must include in the parentheses is the name of the shape, followed by x coordinate, y coordinate and then the speed of the move.

END OF SECTION CHALLENGE

Write a program that includes the following:

-GraphicsWindow.BrushColor,
-GraphicsWindow.DrawEllipse,
-GraphicsWindow.FillEllipse,
-GraphicsWindow.FillTriangle,
-GraphicsWindow.FillRectangle,
-Shapes.AddTriangle, and
-Shapes.Animate.

SECTION THIRTEEN
SUBROUTINES

A subroutine is a set of computer instructions, to be used by a main computer program, that performs some task that you may want to do over and over again at various times. The main computer program could do some of its own actions in a specific sequence, then ask the subroutine to do its tasks, and then continue on where it was before it asked the subroutine to do its tasks. Another term for this is a subprogram (a term we discussed earlier in this book).

EXAMPLE: Within a computer program used to operate a college, there could be a subprogram that checked to see if any new students had been enrolled since you last used the program. The main program could use that subprogram as it was starting up, get the data on any new students, and then continue on with its primary functions.

To "call" means to demand or direct something. In normal English this could be used like, "This calls for celebration!" In computers, a call is a direction by a main computer program to execute the tasks of a subprogram. More specifically, when a "call" is made, a program temporarily transfers control of the computer to a subprogram. Once the subprogram is done executing, control of the computer is returned to the main program. A program could make many "calls" to multiple subprograms as the program does its sequence of tasks.

EXAMPLE: If you were using a video game program, the video game program could call a "high score" subprogram after every game ended.

In Small Basic, the name of a subroutine is preceded with the statement "Sub". The instructions that make up the subroutine end off with the statement "EndSub".

Write and execute the following code:

```
TextWindow.Write("What is your name?: ")
Name = TextWindow.Read()
TextWindow.Write("Hi there, " + Name + "! What time do you think it is? ")
Time = TextWindow.Read()
TextWindow.Write("Well " + Name + ", per your computer, the time now is actually: ")
PrintTime()
Sub PrintTime
  TextWindow.WriteLine(Clock.Time)
EndSub
```

You execute a subroutine by calling the subroutine name followed by (). The parentheses tell the computer that the main program wants a subroutine executed.

In a larger program, subroutines become quite useful and save you from writing extra code because you can call the subroutine from anywhere in the program.

Subroutines can also be used to break apart larger problems into smaller problems.

An important thing to keep in mind in writing code is the readability of your code. I.e. If another developer takes over after you, they need to know the purpose of different sections of your code. To clarify our code, we use "comments." For example: PrintTime() *'this is a subroutine that prints the current time*

This is called "commenting your code."

In Small Basic, comments are preceded with an apostrophe ('). Comments are ignored by the computer and not executed.

To comment the code we wrote above, we would do the following:

```
TextWindow.Write("What is your name?: ") 'This allows the user to enter their name
Name = TextWindow.Read() 'This assigns what the user types to the variable Name
TextWindow.Write("Hi there, " + Name + "! What time do you think it is? ") 'This prints
text and allows the user to guess the time
Time = TextWindow.Read() 'This assigns what the user types to the variable Time
TextWindow.Write("Well " + Name + ", per your computer, the time now is actually: ")
'This prints text
PrintTime() 'This names the subroutine
Sub PrintTime 'This starts the subroutine
  TextWindow.WriteLine(Clock.Time) 'This accesses the computer's clock and returns the
time
EndSub 'This ends the subroutine
```

END OF SECTION CHALLENGE

Write your own program that includes a subroutine, and comment your code.

SECTION FOURTEEN
TURTLES

Write and execute the following code:

```
Turtle.Show()
```

We bet the name of this section makes sense now!

You can move the turtle by entering in numbers inside parentheses (1 means that the Turtle moves 1 pixel; Turtle.Move(50) means that the turtle moves 50 pixels).

Write and execute the following code:

```
Turtle.Move(50)
Program.Delay(500)
Turtle.Move(25)
Program.Delay(500)
Turtle.Move(75)
Program.Delay(500)
Turtle.Move(35)
Program.Delay(500)
```

Now let's have the turtle draw a triangle.

Write and execute the following code:

```
Turtle.Angle = 45
Turtle.Move(150)
Turtle.Angle = 135
Turtle.Move(150)
Turtle.Angle = 270
```

We can also have him turn right or left and change the colors. We will now make a rectangle with the turtle.

Write and execute the following code:

```
GraphicsWindow.BackgroundColor = "LightYellow"
GraphicsWindow.PenColor = "Magenta"
Turtle.Move(100)
Turtle.TurnRight()
Turtle.Move(200)
Turtle.TurnRight()
Turtle.Move(100)
```

```
Turtle.TurnRight()
Turtle.Move(200)
```

We can also draw shapes using a for loop. Let's do an octagon.

Write and execute the following code:

```
For X = 1 To 8
 Turtle.Move(75)
 Turtle.Turn(45)
EndFor
```

Let's make a shape that's virtually a circle. We will also use the X and Y Coordinates to place the turtle where we want it in the Graphics Window. And, to make it more fun, let's randomize some colors! It's about to get trippy…

Write and execute the following code:

```
Turtle.X = 20
Turtle.Y = 200
Sides = 200
Angle = 360 / Sides
Size = 1000 / Sides
For A = 1 To Sides
 GraphicsWindow.PenColor = GraphicsWindow.GetRandomColor()
 GraphicsWindow.BackgroundColor = GraphicsWindow.GetRandomColor()
 Turtle.Move(Size)
 Turtle.Turn(Angle)
EndFor
```

END OF SECTION CHALLENGE 1

Using what you learned so far, have the turtle make a square using a For Loop. Additionally, have a background color, a pen color and try to make the square as centered as you can.

END OF SECTION CHALLENGE 2

Write a program that includes the following:

-Turtle.Show,
-Turtle.Move,
-Turtle.TurnRight,
-Turtle.Angle,
-Turtle.TurnLeft, and
-Turtle.MoveTo.

SECTION FIFTEEN
MORE SUBROUTINES

We can also use subroutines to handle variables.

Write and execute the following code:

```
TextWindow.Write("Type a number: ")
Number_1 = TextWindow.ReadNumber()
TextWindow.Write("Type another number: ")
Number_2 = TextWindow.ReadNumber()
TextWindow.Write("Let's type another number: ")
Number_3 = TextWindow.ReadNumber()
TextWindow.Write("And one last number: ")
Number_4 = TextWindow.ReadNumber()
Largest_Number()
TextWindow.WriteLine("The largest number is: " + Largest_Number)
Sub Largest_Number
 If Number_1 > (Number_2 + Number_3 + Number_4) Then
 Largest_Number = Number_1
 ElseIf Number_2 > (Number_1 + Number_3 + Number_4) Then
 Largest_Number = Number_2
 ElseIf Number_3 > (Number_1 + Number_2 + Number_4) Then
 Largest_Number = Number_3
 Else
 Largest_Number = Number_4
 EndIf
EndSub
```

Now let's try another subprogram that will be called three times.

Write and execute the following subprogram:

```
TextWindow.BackgroundColor = "DarkRed"
TextWindow.Write("This is a program that allows you to choose from various sounds
you'd wish to hear. You'll get to choose three times! ")
Sound()
Sub Sound
Start:
TextWindow.Write("To hear a bell ring, type Bell. To hear a chime, type Chime. To
hear a click sound, type Click: ")
Sound_Choice = TextWindow.Read()
  If Sound_Choice = "Bell" Then
    Sound.PlayBellRing()
  ElseIf Sound_Choice = "Chime" Then
```

```
    Sound.PlayChime()
  ElseIf Sound_Choice = "Click" Then
    Sound.PlayClick()
    Else
      TextWindow.Write("Please type Chime, Bell or Click.")
      Goto Start
  EndIf
EndSub
Sound()
Sound()
```

END OF SECTION CHALLENGE

Create a subroutine that includes variables.

SECTION SIXTEEN
ARRAYS

An array is a collection of data, arranged in rows and columns. In computers, an array is a group of related things that are stored together in a sequence. It is a way things can be organized in a computer in a logical way. Arrays can be quite simple, or quite complex.

EXAMPLE: A simple array would be something like the numbers 7, 3 and 15. It would be written out like this:

[7,3,15]

These three pieces of data are called elements – they are the elements of the array.

A system is needed for identifying each element of an array. The simplest method for this is to start numbering them at zero starting at the left position and count up from there.

In the above example, the element "7" would be at position 0, "3" would be at position 1 and "15" would be at position 2.

Another word for the position of an element is the "index" of the element – for the above example of an array, index 0 is "7", index 1 is "3", etc. The plural form if "index" is "indices", pronounced "IN-dih-sees".

Each element, therefore, has two properties: its index and its value.

EXAMPLE: You have three pictures of your cat and you could save them in an array: CatPic1, CatPic2 and CatPic3. Here, index 1 has a value of "CatPic2".

In some computer languages, including SmallBasic, the index for an element in an array can be a unique text item, instead of a number.

Example:

You could have an array with three elements: 4, 22, 8

The indices for these elements could be:

"planes"
"trains"
"automobiles"

Here, the element in the array with the index "trains" would have a value of 22.

Write and execute the following code:

```
TextWindow.Write("Enter the name for User 1: ")
User_1_Name = TextWindow.Read()
TextWindow.Write("How old is User 1?: ")
User_1_Age = TextWindow.Read()
TextWindow.Write("Enter the name for User 2: ")
User_2_Name = TextWindow.Read()
TextWindow.Write("How old is User 2?: ")
User_2_Age = TextWindow.Read()
TextWindow.Write("Enter the name for User 3: ")
User_3_Name = TextWindow.Read()
TextWindow.Write("How old is User 3?: ")
User_3_Age = TextWindow.Read()
TextWindow.Write("Enter the name for User 4: ")
User_4_Name = TextWindow.Read()
TextWindow.Write("How old is User 4?: ")
User_4_Age = TextWindow.Read()
TextWindow.Write("Greetings Users! ")
TextWindow.Write(User_1_Name + ", you are " + User_1_Age + " years old! ")
TextWindow.Write(User_2_Name + ", you are " + User_2_Age + " years old! ")
TextWindow.Write(User_3_Name + ", you are " + User_3_Age + " years old! ")
TextWindow.Write(User_4_Name + ", you are " + User_4_Age + " years old! ")
```

We can utilize an array to replace having to create the variables User_1_Name, User_1_Age, User_2_Name, User_2_Age, User_3_Name, User_3_Age, User_4_Name and User_4_Age. Instead we can use an index to store the names and ages.

Each of these are indices for the array and are stored as one variable. Storing values in an array allows you to access arrays inside of loops.

Now, let's change this code into an array.

Write and execute the following code:

```
For A = 1 To 4
 TextWindow.WriteLine("Please enter the name for User " + A + ":")
 Name[A] = TextWindow.Read()
EndFor
For B = 1 To 4
 TextWindow.WriteLine("What is User " + B + "'s age?:")
 Age[B] = TextWindow.Read()
EndFor
```

```
TextWindow.Write("Hello ")
For A = 1 To 4
 TextWindow.Write(Name[A])
 If A < 3 Then
  TextWindow.Write(", ")
 ElseIf A < 4 Then
  TextWindow.Write(" and ")
 EndIf
EndFor
TextWindow.Write(". You are ")
For B = 1 To 4
 TextWindow.Write(Age[B])
 If B < 3 Then
  TextWindow.Write(", ")
 ElseIf B < 4 Then
  TextWindow.Write(" and ")
  Else
   TextWindow.Write(" respectively.")
 EndIf
EndFor
TextWindow.WriteLine("")
```

In the above code, "A" and "B" are referred to as the operators. Our indices are 1 to 4 and visually would look something like this:

Indices	1	2	3	4
A (Name)	Name entered by user	Name entered by user	Name entered by user	Name entered by user
B (Age)	Age entered by user	Age entered by user	Age entered by user	Age entered by user

Let's write another array.

Write and execute the following code:

```
TextWindow.Write("What is your name?: ")
Input["Name"] = TextWindow.Read()
TextWindow.Write("How tall are you?: ")
Input["Height"] = TextWindow.Read()
TextWindow.Write("What year were you born?: ")
Input["Birth_year"] = TextWindow.Read()
TextWindow.Write("What is your favorite color?: ")
Input["Color"] = TextWindow.Read()
```

```
TextWindow.Write("What country were you born in?: ")
Input["Country"] = TextWindow.Read()
TextWindow.Write("Please type one of the following to pull relevant data: Name,
Height, Birth_year, Color or Country. ")
Index = TextWindow.Read()
TextWindow.WriteLine("The " + Index + " you entered is " + Input[Index] + "!")
```

To fully understand arrays, you must know what a "data structure" is. A data structure refers to the organization of related pieces of information. There are different data structures that each allow different operations to be performed on the data. A data structure refers to how the data is organized in terms of implementation (use of the data; relation of the various parts of the data). It is a particular way to organize data in a computer so that it can be used efficiently.

Data structures are used as a means of organizing information in a computer so that the data can be utilized in an efficient manner.

EXAMPLE: Consider two different areas of business: The shipping industry and the manufacturing industry.

The types of data the shipping industry may need to collect and organize will center around vehicles and their capacity, shipping rates, fuel costs, travel times between various geographical points, etc.

The types of data the manufacturing industry may need to collect and organize will center around raw materials, product manufacturing methods and times, inventory locations and amounts, shipping information, etc.

The structure of the data used by computers in these two industries may have similarities, but it's certain that the data structures won't be identical.

A linear data structure is simply a data structure where the data in the structure are organized one after the other – basically, a list.

EXAMPLE: A list of the states in the U.S. Each element of the structure, conceptually, comes right before or after another element.

When speaking about arrays, "dimension" has a specific meaning. A one-dimensional array is a linear data structure. The last program we wrote was a one-dimensional array.

A two-dimensional array is basically an array of arrays. Essentially, you could think of this as a grid of rows and columns, where each entry in the grid is itself an array. You will explore this in the next section.

END OF SECTION CHALLENGE

Create your own one-dimensional array.

SECTION SEVENTEEN
TWO-DIMENSIONAL ARRAYS

We will now write a two-dimensional array.

Write and execute the following code:

```
Animals["Princess"]["Color"] = "Black"
Animals["Princess"]["Species"] = "Dog
Animals["Ivy"]["Color"] = "Gray with dark spots and stripes"
Animals["Ivy"]["Species"] = "Cat"
Animals["Goldie"]["Color"] = "Gold"
Animals["Goldie"]["Species"] = "Fish"
Animals["Tweet"]["Color"] = "Green with yellow"
Animals["Tweet"]["Species"] = "Bird"
TextWindow.Write("What is the name?: ")
Name = TextWindow.Read()
TextWindow.WriteLine("Their color is: " + Animals[Name]["Color"])
TextWindow.WriteLine("Their species is: " + Animals[Name]["Species"])
```

When the program runs, it will ask you for the name of the pet. Enter one of the four names (Princess, Ivy, Goldie or Tweet).

Visually, this is what we created in our array:

Name:	Princess	Ivy	Goldie	Tweet
Color:	Black	Gray with dark spots and stripes	Gold	Green with yellow
Species:	Dog	Cat	Goldfish	Parakeet

Arrays can also be used with Graphics.

Write and execute the following code:

```
GraphicsWindow.BackgroundColor = "Black"
GraphicsWindow.Height = 600
GraphicsWindow.Width = 605
Rows = 10
Columns = 10
Sides = 50
For A = 1 To Columns
 For B = 1 To Rows
  GraphicsWindow.BrushColor = "Blue"
```

```
    Squares[A][B] = Shapes.AddRectangle(Sides, Sides)
    Shapes.Move(Squares[A][B], A * Sides, B * Sides)
  EndFor
EndFor
```

END OF SECTION CHALLENGE

Create your own two-dimensional array.

SECTION EIGHTEEN
SOME BASIC PROGRAMS

Now we will put together some of what you've learned so far to make some basic programs. Actually type out all code in the Editor – this is vital experience for you as a developer. Feel free to customize some of these programs if you choose.

PROGRAM 1

```
GraphicsWindow.BackgroundColor = "LightCyan"
GraphicsWindow.PenColor = "DarkSlateBlue"
GraphicsWindow.Width = 400
GraphicsWindow.Height = 400
For A = 1 To 200 Step 6
 GraphicsWindow.DrawRectangle(200 - A, 200 - A, A * 2, A * 2)
 Program.Delay(100)
 EndFor
For A = 1 To 200 Step 6
 GraphicsWindow.DrawEllipse(200 - A, 200 - A, A * 2, A *2)
 Program.Delay(100)
EndFor
```

PROGRAM 2

```
GraphicsWindow.Width = 1000
GraphicsWindow.Height = 650
GraphicsWindow.BackgroundColor = "Black"
A = 1000
B = 1000
For C = 1 To 100000
 D = Math.GetRandomNumber(3)
 E = 500
 Program.Delay(.1)
 F = 30
 If (D = 1) then
  E = 30
  Program.Delay(.1)
  F = 1000
 EndIf
 If (D = 2) Then
  E = 1000
  F = 1000
  Program.Delay(.1)
 EndIf
 A = (A + E) / 2
```

```
 Program.Delay(.1)
 B = (B + F) / 2
 Random_Color = GraphicsWindow.GetRandomColor()
 GraphicsWindow.SetPixel(A, B, Random_Color)
EndFor
```

PROGRAM 3

```
GraphicsWindow.Title = "America!"
GraphicsWindow.Width = 1000
GraphicsWindow.Height = 600
For A = 1 To 100000
 GraphicsWindow.BrushColor = "Red"
 B = Math.GetRandomNumber(1000)
 C = Math.GetRandomNumber(1000)
 GraphicsWindow.FillEllipse(B, C, 4, 4)
EndFor
For D = 1 To 100000
 GraphicsWindow.BrushColor = "Blue"
 B = Math.GetRandomNumber(500)
 C = Math.GetRandomNumber(275)
 GraphicsWindow.FillEllipse(B, C, 4, 4)
EndFor
```

PROGRAM 4

```
GraphicsWindow.Width = 275
Turtle.X = 130
Turtle.Y = 400
GraphicsWindow.PenColor = "Green"
Turtle.Move(150)
Turtle.X = 135
Turtle.Y = 400
GraphicsWindow.PenColor = "Green"
Turtle.Move(150)
Turtle.X = 100
Turtle.Y = 200
GraphicsWindow.PenColor = "MediumVioletRed"
Turns = 200
Length = 300 /  Turns
Angle = 400 / Turns
Turtle.Speed = 10
For A = 1 To 6
 For B = 1 To Turns
  Turtle.Move(Length)
```

```
    Turtle.Turn(Angle)
  EndFor
  Turtle.Turn(18)
EndFor
Turtle.X = 128.5
Turtle.Y = 193
```

PROGRAM 5

```
GraphicsWindow.BackgroundColor = "DarkBlue"
GraphicsWindow.Height = 600
GraphicsWindow.Width = 605
Rows = 10
Columns = 10
Sides = 50
For A = 1 To Columns
  For B = 1 To Rows
    GraphicsWindow.BrushColor = GraphicsWindow.GetRandomColor()
    Squares[A][B] = Shapes.AddRectangle(Sides, Sides)
    Shapes.Move(Squares[A][B], A * Sides, B * Sides)
  EndFor
EndFor
For A = 1 To Columns
  For B = 1 To Rows
    Shapes.Animate(Squares[B][A], 300, 0, 1000)
    Program.Delay(50)
  EndFor
EndFor
For A = 1 To Columns
  For B = 1 To Rows
    Shapes.Animate(Squares[B][A], 288, 500, 1000)
    Program.Delay(10)
  EndFor
EndFor
For A = 1 To Columns
  For B = 1 To Rows
    Shapes.Animate(Squares[B][A], 275, 250, 1000)
    Program.Delay(10)
  EndFor
EndFor
```

SECTION NINETEEN
EVENTS

An event is an action or something that occurs that is detected by a computer program. There can be system events (events that occur as a result of operations the computer does automatically), or user events, like typing on the keyboard or clicking a mouse.

In Small Basic, an event is something that reacts to a user's action and is when the computer tells you that something interesting has happened. For example, if you make a program that turns the screen blue when you click on the word "blue," clicking on the word "blue" would be the event.

Events can make programs more interesting and interactive.

Interactive means that two things influence one another and create effects on each other. In computers, interactive refers to a computer that is able to be communicated with and gotten to perform activities by a human; these activities involve the person using the computer. An interactive computer is a computer that you can affect in some way (move a pointer on a screen and select something, etc.) and which will respond in some manner. Most, if not all, computers you've handled have been interactive.

The computer game "Hangman" could be developed in Small Basic and would include events. In this game, the user makes choices and the program receives the user's input using events.

There is such a thing as "event-driven programming." This is programming where the flow of the program is controlled by events. An example would be a program in which the program flow is determined by the typing of keys and clicking the mouse.

We will now use the MouseDown event in the following program (you will see what it does when you run the program). We can pull a picture from Flickr!

Write and execute the following code:

```
GraphicsWindow.Title = "It's raining cats and dogs!"
GraphicsWindow.Width = 700
GraphicsWindow.Height = 700
GraphicsWindow.MouseDown = Pics
Sub Pics
  Picture = Flickr.GetRandomPicture("Cats, Dogs")
  GraphicsWindow.DrawResizedImage(Picture, 0, 0, 700, 700)
EndSub
```

We just used a new operation called "DrawResizedImage" which allows you to display photos. The first word in the parentheses names the picture, the next two numbers are the X and Y Coordinates in the Graphics Window and the last two specify the width and length of the photo (respectively). Let's get a little tougher on events.

Write and execute the following code:

```
GraphicsWindow.DrawBoundText(250, 200, 100, "Click the screen!")
GraphicsWindow.MouseDown = Click
GraphicsWindow.BrushColor = "Yellow"
GraphicsWindow.BackgroundColor = "Black"
Sub Click
 GraphicsWindow.ShowMessage("You clicked the mouse!", "NOTICE")
 A = GraphicsWindow.MouseX - 5
 B = GraphicsWindow.MouseY - 5
GraphicsWindow.FillTriangle(A, B, 30, 30, 40, 40)
EndSub
```

There are two chunks of text following ShowMessage. The first chunk is what will be displayed inside the window, and the second chunk is what is displayed at the top.

This program contains a subroutine as well. Every time the user clicks in the GraphicsWindow, the subroutine "Click" is called. The Click subroutine results in a couple events: 1. A message pops up and 2. A yellow ray expands out from the top left corner after you shut the message box. One of the unique things about events is that when an event occurs, the subroutine is called automatically.

In the above code, we assigned the subroutine name to the MouseDown event which is connected to the GraphicsWindow object. Even though the MouseDown looks like a property (attributes of an object), we are actually assigning the subroutine "Click" to it. If MouseDown were a property, we would be assigning it a value (as opposed to a subroutine).

Now that you are familiar with subroutines, events and other key coding concepts, we can create our very own "Paint" program that will allow you to draw using the mouse. You will be able to draw in rainbow-like colors with a thick brush.

In this next program, we will be using the MouseMove event, which gets the X and Y coordinates, in pixels, of the mouse cursor – based on where it is as compared to the top left of the desktop.

Write and execute the following code:

```
GraphicsWindow.MouseMove = A
GraphicsWindow.MouseDown = B
GraphicsWindow.BackgroundColor = "SkyBlue"
GraphicsWindow.PenWidth = (25)
Sub B
 C = GraphicsWindow.MouseX
 D = GraphicsWindow.MouseY
EndSub
Sub A
 E = GraphicsWindow.MouseX
 F = GraphicsWindow.MouseY
 If (Mouse.IsLeftButtonDown) Then
  GraphicsWindow.PenColor = GraphicsWindow.GetRandomColor()
  GraphicsWindow.DrawLine(C, D, E, F)
 EndIf
C = E
D = F
EndSub
'Click and hold down mouse as you move it around.
```

END OF SECTION CHALLENGE

Create a program that includes the following events:

-MouseUp,
-MouseDown,
-MouseMove,
-KeyDown, and
-KeyUp.

SECTION TWENTY
THE FINAL SECTION

We will now do some coding exercises that may require you to do some online research.

SMALL BASIC EXERCISE 1

HERE IS YOUR ASSIGNMENT: Create a program that returns the smaller of two numbers entered by a user. The program should receive two different numbers chosen by the user and then display the smaller of the two.

For example: The user inputs 21 and 3 and the program returns the number 3.

Hint: If statements

SMALL BASIC EXERCISE 2

The company you work for just opened two new branches. One is in New York City, the other in London. They need a very simple program to find out if the branches are open or closed based on the current time of the Headquarters here in Portland. The hours of both branches are 9:00 a.m.-9:00 p.m. in their own time zone.

HERE IS YOUR ASSIGNMENT: Create a program that will determine whether the London and New York offices are open or closed based on the current time of the HQ in Portland. Have the program display if each of the two branches are open or closed.

Hints: Clock.Time class (Clock.Hour operates on a 24-hour clock)

If statements

SMALL BASIC EXERCISE 3

Your employer wants a program to copy a .txt file from one folder to another.

HERE IS YOUR ASSIGNMENT: Create two folders on your desktop. Create one text file inside one of the folders (leaving the other folder empty).

Your task is to use Small Basic to copy the file from the folder it is stored in and place the copy in the empty folder.

Note: In Windows, to obtain the file path, hold shift and right click on the file and then choose "copy as path"

Hint: File.CopyFile Method

SMALL BASIC EXERCISE 4

Your employer now wants a program that will copy a .txt file from one folder to another only if the London office is closed.

HERE IS YOUR ASSIGNMENT: Using the same two folders created in Exercise 3, make a program that copies a file from the folder it is stored in and place it in the other folder ONLY if the London office is closed.

Hint: It's okay to re-use code you wrote in Exercises 2 and 3.

SMALL BASIC EXERCISE 5

Your employer loves the program you just created, but now wants it to have a simple graphical user interface (GUI) for other employees to use. Note: a GUI is a representation of the various objects in a computer – files, programs, etc. - in a graphical form. That is, it presents the user with pictures and diagrams that communicate the things on the computer, and their arrangement.

HERE IS YOUR ASSIGNMENT: Make a simple GUI for your program. All it needs to have is a button in the middle that, when clicked, copies a file from one folder to another ONLY if the London office is closed.

Hint: Make the code you wrote in Exercise 4 a subroutine that is called when a button is clicked.

THE END

CONGRATULATIONS! You've completed The Tech Academy's "Learn Coding Basics in Hours with Small Basic" book!

Well done on persisting through this book! Not only have you learned Small Basic (a great beginner's programming language, and a wonderful undercut to learning .NET), you have also been trained in several key programming concepts that apply to *all* programming languages.

As the next step, we recommend enrolling in our Software Developer Boot Camp. The Tech Academy creates well-rounded, entry-level developers.

Visit: learncodinganywhere.com!